Disney Winnie the Pooh

How Does Your Garden Grow?

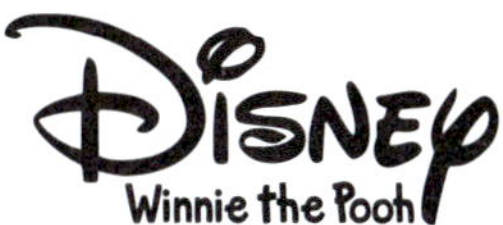

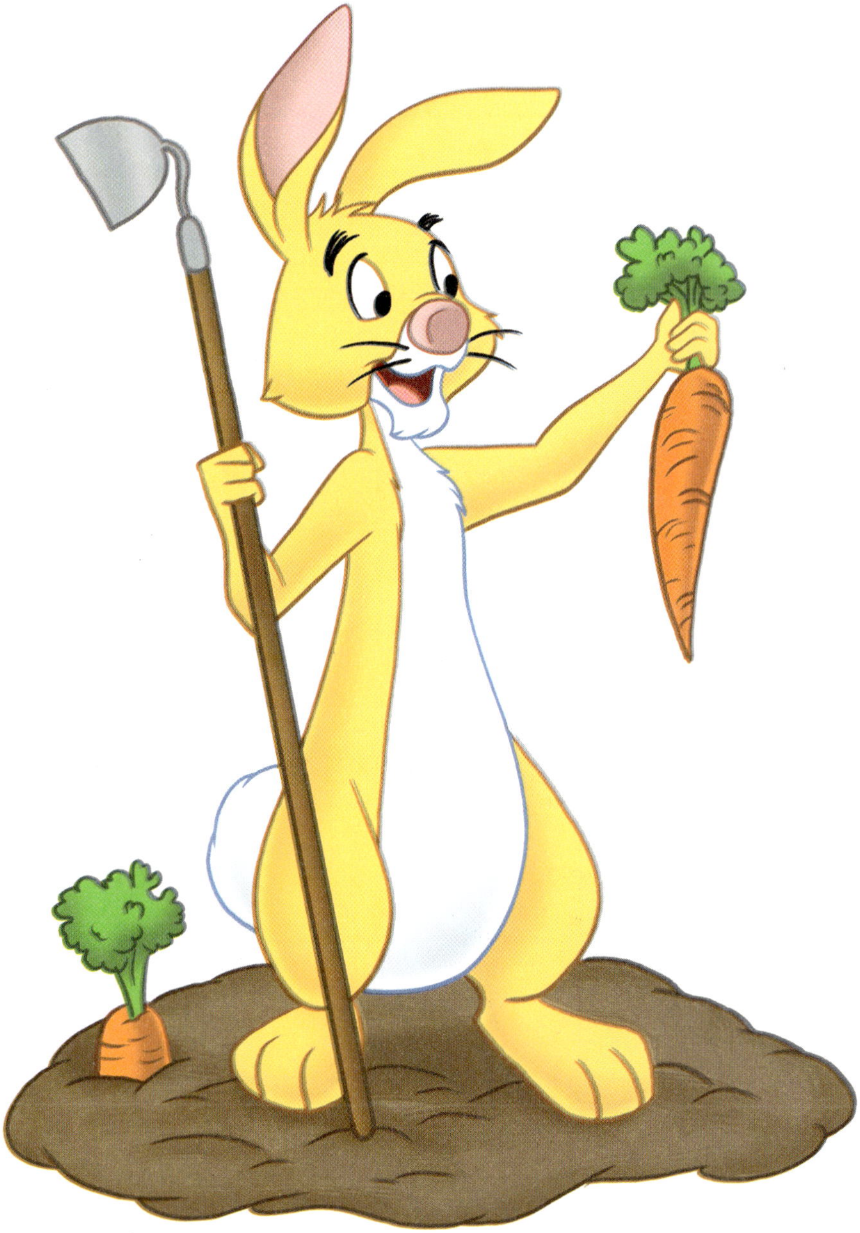

MW01620559

"There's a buzz in the air," said Pooh happily. "And buzzing means honey."

So he followed the sound, hoping it would lead to a hive. Instead it led to Rabbit's garden where everyone was admiring his vegetables.

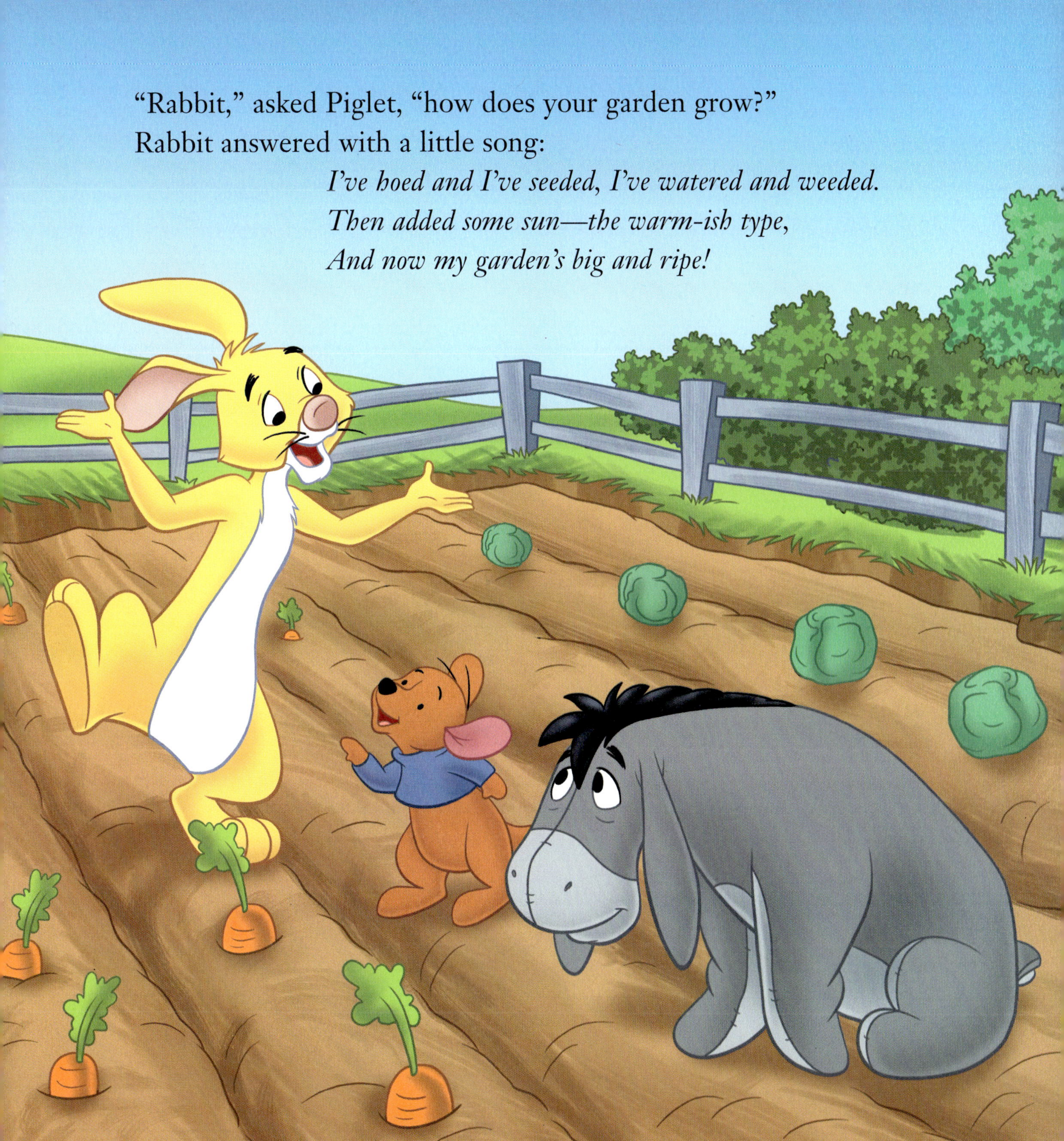

“Rabbit,” asked Piglet, “how does your garden grow?”

Rabbit answered with a little song:

I’ve hoed and I’ve seeded, I’ve watered and weeded.
Then added some sun—the warm-ish type,
And now my garden’s big and ripe!

“What a corntastic song!” said Tigger excitedly. “But what does it mean?”

“It means my hard work has finally paid off,” said Rabbit proudly. “Come inside and have some homemade vegetable soup.”

Watching the bees through the window, Pooh got an idea. “If I planted a flower garden, perhaps the bees might visit me, and where there are bees...there is honey!”

"I suppose," said Rabbit. "But growing a garden is a lot of work, and it takes patience."

"That's okay, Rabbit," said Pooh. "It'll be easier on my fluff and stuff than climbing trees for honey."

"Have it your way," said Rabbit, smiling. "Good luck!"

"I can almost hear the bees buzzing," said Pooh as he scattered seeds around his house. He waited and watched all afternoon, but no flowers grew.

Pooh knew there were lovely flowers growing in his Thinking Spot. He decided to visit them to see if he could figure out how they grew.

The next day everyone came by to see how Pooh's garden was coming along.

"I'm afraid I don't have a green thumb," said Pooh sadly, "just a sticky paw."

"Well, Pooh, there *is* a science to gardening," said Rabbit. "Let me show you how it's done."

Rabbit explained the first thing needed was a sunny spot.

"How about here?" asked Pooh, standing by his kitchen window.

"Stupenderous!" said Tigger.

"Rabbit," asked Roo, "why do plants need sun?"

"Excellent question!" said Rabbit. "The sun gives plants energy which they need to grow."

“Secondly, you need to dig holes like this,” said Rabbit. Everyone pulled his hoe across the ground and scooped out some soil. “Now drop in the seed and cover it with the soil you scooped out.”

“Can we plant some seeds in my Sandy Pit?” asked Roo hopefully.